How to ride a horse

Debbie Burgermeister

Copyright © 2019

The moral right of Debbie Burgermeister to be identified as the author
and Meftahul Amin to be identified as the cover illustrator
has been asserted by them in accordance with the Copyright, Design and
Patents Act 1988.

All rights reserved. No part of this book may be reproduced or
transmitted in any form or by any means, electronic or mechanical,
including photocopying, recording, or by any information storage and
retrieval system, without permission in writing from the copyright owner,
except for the inclusion of brief quotations in a review.

 A catalogue record for this book is available from the National Library of Australia

ISBN: 9780648743712

Book creation, editing, design and layout by Crazy Diamond Publishing
Print and channel distribution: Lightning Source / Ingram
Publisher: Horse Riding Hub

www.horseridinghub.com

DISCLAIMER: "All content, including text, graphics, images and
information, contained on or available through this book is for general
information purposes only. Such information is subject to change without
notice. You are encouraged to confirm any information obtained from or
through this book with other sources and professionals."

This lesson book belongs to:

_____

Lesson Modules

LESSON 1

Introduction to Horse Safety   1

Introduction to Horse Riding Skills 1   3

- Mount and dismount
- Hold reins correctly (shorten and lengthen)
- Walk straight, turn and stop

LESSON 2

Introduction to Horse Riding Skills 2   7

- Walk circles / hand and leg aids
- Changing direction through figure of eight

LESSON 3

Introduction to Horse Handling 1   11

- Moving around the horse and brushing its body
- Leading your horse

Horse Riding skills – Practice and Perfection   13

- Figure of eight / The art of hand and leg aids balance
- Theory in trotting

LESSON 4

Introduction to Horse Riding Skills 3   17

- Learn to trot – basic

LESSON 5

Introduction to Horse Handling 2   **22**

- Put halter and bridle on
- Put saddle on and adjust girth from ground and saddle

Introduction to Horse Riding Skills 4   **24**

- The art of rise trot
- Learn about diagonals

LESSON 6

Introduction to Horse Riding Skills 5   **27**

- Turns and corners / Changing rein at walk and trot

Introduction to Horse Riding Skills 6

- Preparation for the canter

LESSON 7

Horse Riding Skills – Practice and Perfection   **34**

- Introduction to Sit Trot and Cantering

LESSON 8

Introduction to Horse Riding Skills 7   **36**

- Riding without Stirrups

LESSON 9

Horse Riding Skills Refresher   **41**

LESSON 10
Horse Saddlery Parts   44

LESSON 11
Horse Care   48
- Parts of the body
- Your horse and you
- Grooming kit essentials

LESSON 12
Horse Riding Skills Checklist   53

LESSON 13
Your Horse and You   56

LESSON 14
What Next?   66
- Intermediate and Advanced Riding Skills
- Advanced Horse Care
- Horsemanship and Training

Horse Pathway Development Guide   68
- An overview of your horse goals and achievements to work towards along your journey

About the Author   77

How to ride a horse

Lesson 1

Module – Introduction to Horse Safety

Horses frighten easily.

There are simple rules to avoid danger around horses:

- always WALK, never run
- avoid loud and sudden noises

Horses display anger or show they are scared when:

- their ears go back
- they show the white part of their eye

Never walk too close to horses' back legs as they are big animals and can injure you if they kick.

To avoid startling your horse, talk when approaching and always approach towards the shoulder, the safe zone.

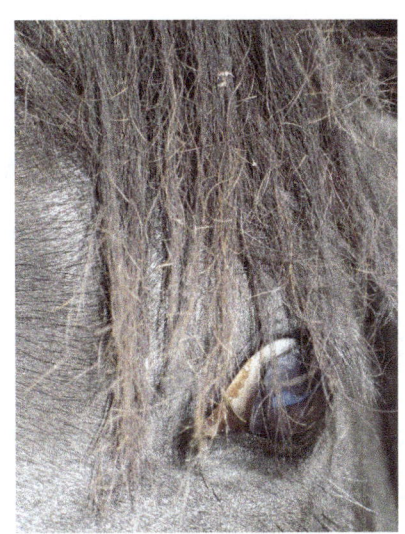

Follow your safety rules. Horses are beautiful creatures and will respond to your firm but kind approach.

Things to remember:

- Be careful and safe

- Be confident and positive

Horses can sense your feelings and try their best to help you. Be firm and kind to your horse. They will respond with trust and willingness.

Module – Introduction to Riding Skills 1

There are just a few simple words to remember that you will hear in all your lessons:

- **Sit up straight**

    ("rabbit ears", shoulders back)

- **Heels down**

    (ball of foot in stirrup only)

- **Hands down**

- **Grip with your thighs and knees, not your ankles**

- **Breathe and relax**

This lesson we are going to learn how to:

- Get on the horse (mounting)
- How to hold the reins correctly and shorten them when riding
- Walk, turn and stop

Giddy Up Beginner Books

How to ride a horse

Notes

Giddy Up Beginner Books

Lesson 1 Review:

The safest area to approach a horse is the sh _ _ lder
The words to remember when riding are:

- He _ ls   down
- Han _ s   _ own
- When turning my horse I use my inside Ha _ d and outside L _ g
- Most of all I need to R _ _ ax

Some things to practice!

Standing with your toes up on something at home for leg stretch and heels down exercise. A rolled up towel or a block.

0 0 0 (brick/plank)

Walking around at home with hand and leg signals needed when riding.

Now you have moved from the pretend horse to the real horse. You can now start to learn some more riding skills.

Lesson 2

Module – Introduction to Horse Riding Skills 2

Focus on walking in a circle and changing direction through a figure of eight.

The importance of hand and leg aids is to give your horse guidance, for the horse to be willing to do what you ask of them.

- Using the inside rein to steer the horse in the correct direction.

- Using your legs to turn is the most important part of riding to ensure you do not pull too much on the horse's delicate mouth.

- Gaining the balance between hands and legs is the "ART of riding".

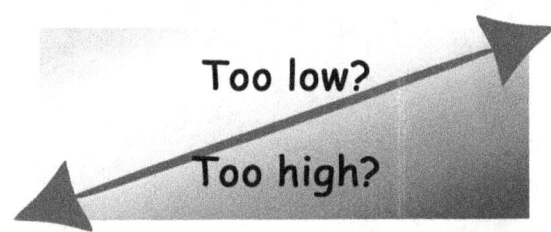

Trotting theory

- What do you need to know before this?

- Make sure your stirrups are the right length to ensure you can rise out of the saddle so you don't bounce around. (Stirrup base at the bottom of your ankle bone is a good tip and standing without your heels coming up.)

- Complete control of the horse before starting to trot. How are you progressing?

Giddy Up Beginner Books

Notes

Lesson 2 Review:

Please draw a figure of eight that you learnt last lesson when changing direction.

- I need to remember when riding to:
    - Keep my elb_ _ _ close to my side
    - Hands d _ wn and Th _ _ bs up
    - The art of horse riding is the correct balance between your l_ _ _ and h _ _ _

Remembering to practice

Walking around at home with something between your elbows and back to remind you of the correct position to hold your arms and hands.

How to ride a horse

Lesson 3

Module – Introduction to Horse Handling 1

Moving around your horse in the safe zone

- Stay close to the shoulders
- Talk to your horse and your hands always on the body to let them know you are there
- Walk around the hind legs to avoid the kicking zone to swap sides

How to brush your horse safely

Different brushes left to right

- soft brush and dandy brush
- mane and tail brush and curry comb

Giddy Up Beginner Books

Let's take your horse for a lead.

• Remember to NEVER loop the rope around your hand. Always fold the lead.

Don't try to pull and have a tug of war with your horse as they may become resistant. Give and take.

Stay at your horse's shoulder and then walk your horse by a slight pull on the lead or moving the horse to the right or left to give your horse indication you want to move forward.

You need to be confident to let them know who's boss. Be kind at the same time so they will be willing to walk by your side.

Horse Riding Skills: Practice and Perfection

Figure of eight – the art of hand and leg aids balance.

8

- Stopping and moving forward
    - Guidance with your hands
    - Direction with leg aids to move forward

- Trotting theory
    - Practice at the walk how to rise out of the saddle so you don't bounce at the trot
    - Position of the hands
    - Balance with the legs
    - Using your hips so you're not jumping out of the saddle from your toes. Can you dance? Understand how your hips and stomach move as that's the secret to your trot.

Giddy Up Beginner Books

Lesson 3 Review:

Practice turning and control of your horse with reins and legs.

Module – Practice Horse Handling

- Brushing your horse
- Leading your horse
- Watch a horse being saddled and bridled

Notes

How to ride a horse

Lesson 4

Module – Introduction to Horse Riding Skills 3

In this lesson we are going to focus on starting to trot.

- Turn, stop and move forward with complete control
- Remember hand and leg commands (aids)
- Shorten and lengthen reins with ease

Try not to let your mind wander away from horse riding – this is very important as you start to trot.

Trotting theory

Make sure your stirrups are the right length to ensure you can rise out of the saddle so you don't bounce around.

Learning to Trot

- Practice at the walk how to rise out of the saddle so you don't bounce at the trot. Count the beat 1-2-1-2-Up-Down-Up-Down.
- Position of the hands.
- Balance with the legs – grip with the knees and thighs and top of your calf.

- Watch how it is done and look at the movement of the hoof beat for rising up and down.

Let's Trot

• Feel and listen to the hoof beat for the speed of the up and down movement.

• Ready to trot... strong grip with the knees, lean forward but keep your feet flat not letting your heels come up, pressure in the stirrup, no need to jump out of the saddle, just rise a little bit and balance.

End of lesson 4 – Time to Relax

What a great stepping stone in your riding. You have now learnt the basics of how to trot! Well done! Have a well earned rest.

Notes

Lesson 5

Module – Introduction to Horse Handling 2

Catch a horse in stable and put halter on

- Don't forget horses have big heads and you can never compete with your horse in strength, so you must use your brain to understand the horse's motives and needs. Learn to interpret it's behaviour.

- Always let your horse know that you are approaching as it could be dozing and get a fright which could cause a kick or bite reaction as natural animal protection.

- Approach your horse from the front just to the side so you are not in danger of front leg striking or back leg kicking.

- Always beware of warning signs such as ears back or turning of the rump. Make sure you behave calmly, clearly and confidently.

- Never place yourself in a position where you cannot get away, and do not sit or kneel down.

Put saddlecloth and saddle on

- Saddlecloth falls in line with the front leg.

- Move to the off side (right side) of your horse to straighten the girth and breastplate if you have one before doing up. Then go back to the near side (left), and do up the girth. Pull the stirrups down also.

- The girth part of the saddle should sit just behind the front leg. Lift saddle forward if needed.

- Lift the saddlecloth slightly so airflow is created under the saddle.
- Move back to the near side (left side) to do up the breastplate first (if you have one), then the girth.

Adjust and tighten girth.

- Do up slowly when first doing up the buckle as you can pinch your horse and it may bite or buck if not ready for such tightness.
- Tighten slightly again to firm.
- Untie your horse and walk around, then tighten girth again.
- Stretch front leg so no girth pinching.
- Check stirrup length by putting the ends of your fingers at the top of the buckle. The correct length is when the stirrup measures to just under your armpit.

Put Bridle on.

- Always put the rope/reins around the neck for control of the horse when putting halter/bridle on. Whatever you are putting on is the control piece that goes around the neck.
- When learning undo the halter and tie back around the horse's neck so it is still tied up while you work out your bridle.
- Right hand then holds top of bridle, throatlash is on the right side, left hand is then flat underneath the bit with the left thumb

inside the bit near the horse's mouth where there are no teeth.

- Do up the throatlash last.

Module – Introduction to Riding Skills 4

Complete control at the trot turning and stopping with ease.

Practice being able to rise up and down to the correct beat with good hand and leg position (arms and hands low and heels down)

Learn about diagonals

- This is what makes your horse balanced and is also much more comfortable when riding your horse in a circle.

- At the trot, when the outside shoulder lifts and goes forward, we rise and, when the outside foot hits the ground, we sit. You can focus on whatever works for you, based on your senses of seeing, feeling and hearing the hoof beat to achieve the correct diagonal.

- When changing direction through the centre of the arena (figure of eight) we sit 2 beats and this changes our diagonal so you are sitting on the outside leg in the new direction.

End of lesson 5 – Time to Relax

Keep up the good work. Horse riding requires patience, confidence and practice. You can rest now.

How to ride a horse

Notes

Lesson 6

Module – Introduction to Horse Riding Skills 5

Trotting with ease, turning corners and changing direction with correct diagonals.

How to turn corners better and smoothly

- The ice cream scoop position with your hand.
- Inside leg pressure on the girth.
- Outside hand and outside leg pressure.

Module – Introduction to Riding Skills 6

Preparation for the Canter: are you ready?

Two point position/jump position standing in your stirrups at the trot without your seat in the saddle.

Introduction to sit trot and achieving good balance.

Modules in Review – progress so far

Horse Care and Safety

SAFETY – You always need to remember the Safe Zone no matter what you are doing around horses. Sometimes you can forget this.

LEADING – Lead your horse so you don't walk too close to the front feet. Keeping the reins "even" held in the right hand for control and left hand to pick up the excess of lead without looping over your hands at any stage. Using your elbow for additional control.

GROOMING – You now know how to brush a horse safely using your hands to let the horse know you are there, talking to your horse and selecting the right brush.

Riding Skills

BALANCE, REIN CONTROL, LEG AIDS – You have learnt the very basics of riding, and now you need to learn new skills to feel comfortable on a horse through different movements and at different speeds.

COMMUNICATION – You can tell the horse is happy to have you on their back when your horse is relaxed with you, ears

How to ride a horse

forward and moving along with ease. You will then have a natural companionship with a horse.

In review:

- How to put the reins over your horse's head ready to ride.

- MOUNT – How to get on as best as possible at your age with help. Using your left hand to hold the reins for control of your horse while mounting.

- Stopping, turning and doing a figure of eight.

Tips to be practicing at home for horse riding to become second nature so you don't have to think so much when on your horse:

- Standing on a brick or roll of carpet at home to strengthen your legs and the feeling of keeping your heels down.

- Stand up straight, roll your shoulders back to create a nice riding position (nice tall rabbit ears).

- Walk in circles at home with your hands moving to the inside and DOWN to develop the habit of "hands down and forward" when riding. (Put a broom handle behind your back with your elbows under it to keep your shoulders back, elbows by your side and hands down).

- Sit on a small chair, stool or bucket and practice standing half way up slowly up and down for developing leg strength for trotting.

Things you now need to focus and concentrate on to build your confidence and gain better horse control:

- Looking straight ahead between your horse's ears when riding. (to anticipate your horse's movements before they do them and give appropriate leg and hand aids beforehand).

- Hands down and arms forward are the biggest things to remember for your balance and getting your horse to relax and move forward freely.

- The balance of hand and leg aids is hard but practice and time will see this improve.

Lesson 6 Review:

Riding Skills: Practice and perfection

Focus on leg strength at the trot to keep heels down, elbows by your side, using your hips and hands down when trotting for good body and horse control.

Not quite ready for the canter yet? Sit trot needs to be achieved.

You need continued practice to concentrate on feeling the direction of the horse for turning corners and changing direction with control.

You are learning the art of rise trot and diagonals.

Giddy Up Beginner Books

End of lesson 6 – Time to Relax

Great work. Practicing and having fun will be the main focus for you now to move forward in your riding skills.

Notes

Lesson 7

Lesson 6 Review:

Strong concentration required on feeling the direction the horse is wanting to go and shortening reins.

Module – Horse Riding Skills – Practice and Perfection

- Focus on achieving a good sit trot
- Legs long, not too much pressure on the stirrup
- Gripping with your knees, thigh, top of calf
- Sitting tall with your chin and chest up

Dropping your lower back in the saddle and using your stomach and hips to stay seated and in rhythm with your horse so you don't bounce.

End of lesson 7

Notes

Lesson 8

Lesson 7 Review:

Last lesson we focused on the sit trot and diagonals.

Module – Introduction to Horse Riding Skills 7

Riding without stirrups

Trying something a bit different today – without stirrups. This will increase your balance for future cantering.

Things to remember:

1. Sit deep in the saddle and don't lean forward.

2. Lean back and up with strong pressure with the thighs at the sit trot.

3. Hang on with the top of your legs, not your hands.

4. Squeeze your thighs and bottom to stay on your horse at the canter. The stomach moves with the horse.

5. Keeps hands low near the shoulders of the horse for balance.

How to ride a horse

6. Elbows by your side.

7. Lifting chest up to sit straight, pushing shoulders down to keep arms and hands low.

8. Back straight and tucking tail bone under to sit deep into the saddle.

9. Knees bent, heels down, toes up and in.

10. Riding our horse with your bottom, thighs and top of calves, this is the KEY to successful horse riding.

The more it feels natural and you don't have to think so much about every movement, the easier it will become.

Lesson 8 Review:

We have now touched on learning to ride without stirrups to gain balance and confidence for progressing your riding and leg strength for trotting.

Showing some great confidence with your balance, your hands in the correct position, nice and low, and starting to give leg aids that your horse can feel when you kick. Well done.

Congratulations on improvement in your trotting. This is a great development in your advancement in riding skills.

PRACTICE = PERFECTION = EASY = FUN

End of lesson 8 – Time to Relax

Notes

Lesson 9

Module – Horse Riding Skills Refresher

Trotting practice

- The importance of gripping with your knees, thighs and top of your calf for balance, gaining better control with both arms and legs at the same time.
- Focus on changing direction and diagonals.

Practice

Remember at home to practice sitting on a stool and standing up and down slowly to build knee and leg strength as well as your BALANCE.

Also important is your flexibility to stretch your hips and legs to enable you to get on your horse easily.

Learning to trot will wear you out, but your legs will build strength and it will all be very rewarding down the track... A well-earned rest.

- Lots of practice to gain balance and correct leg position.

- Perfecting the figure of eight.

- Not quite ready for canter but getting close.

- Need more leg strength to get our horse to move freely.

Notes

Giddy Up Beginner Books

Lesson 10

Module – Horse Saddlery Parts

The halter and bridle. Say hello to Magic.

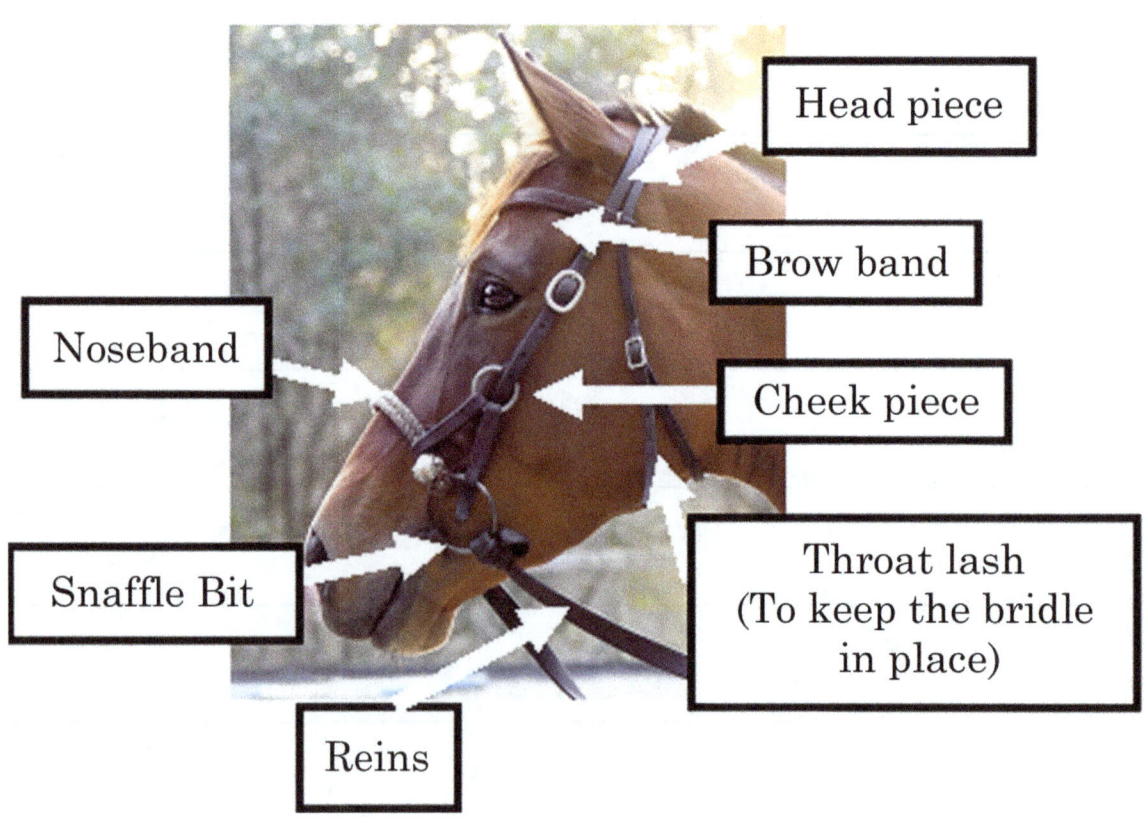

The Saddle

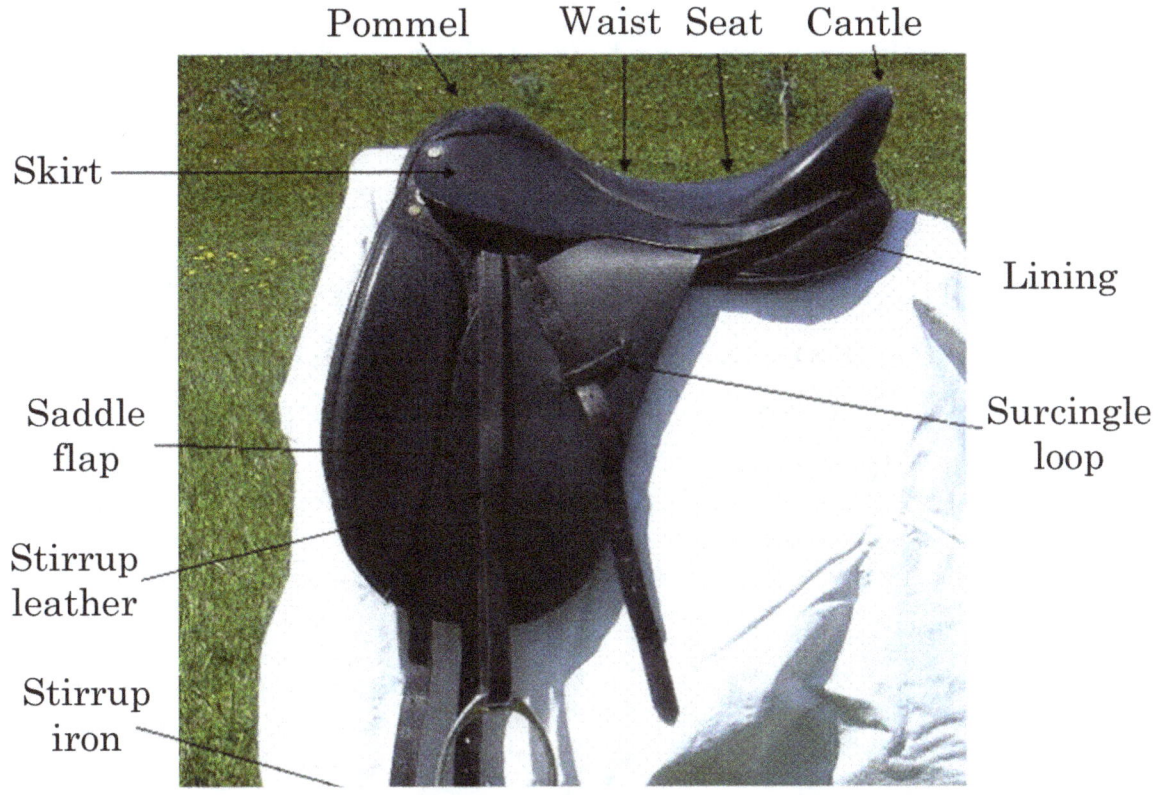

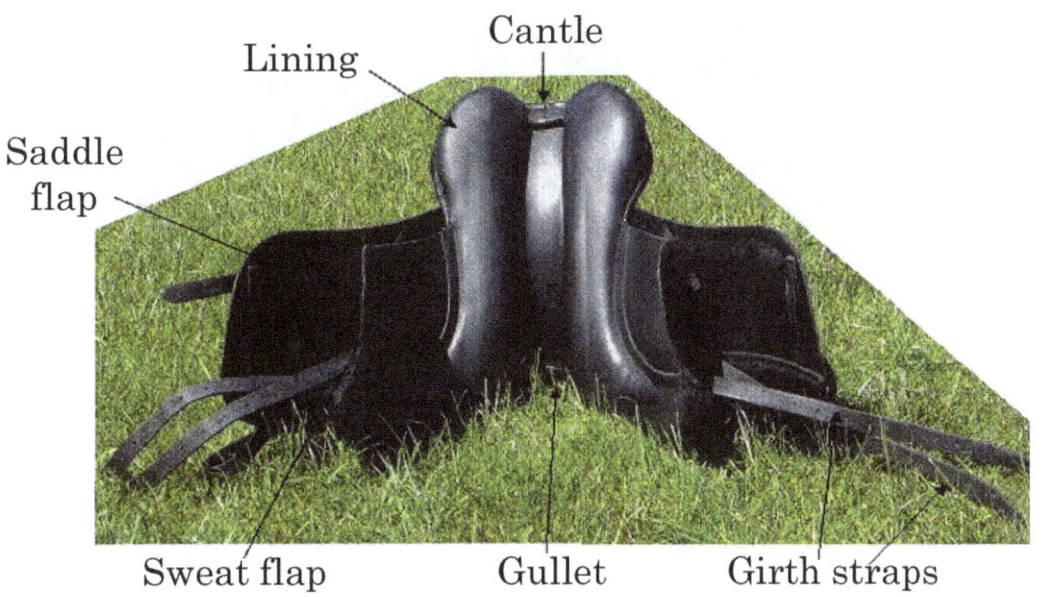

See what you can remember.

Point to the following parts of the bridle and saddle:

Bridle

1. Head piece
2. Brow band
3. Cheek piece
4. Throat lash
5. Snaffle bit
6. Reins
7. Halter
8. Noseband

How to ride a horse

Saddle

1. Seat
2. Waist
3. Cantle
4. Pommel
5. Saddle flap
6. Skirt
7. Lining
8. Stirrup leathers
9. Stirrup iron
10. Sweat flap
11. Gullet
12. Girth
13. Girth buckles and straps

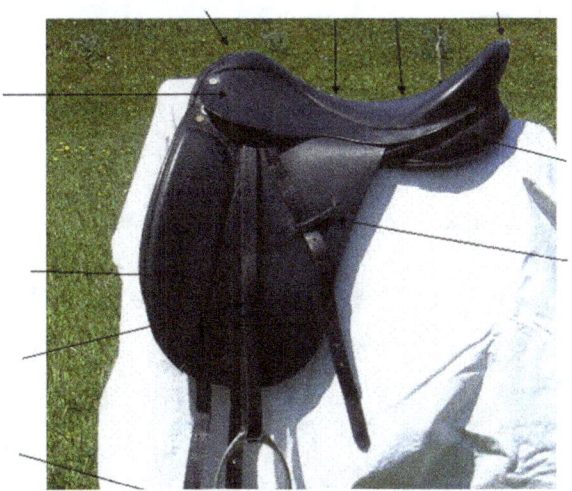

Lesson 11

Module – Horse Care

Parts of the body – Horse Head. Say hello to Casanova.

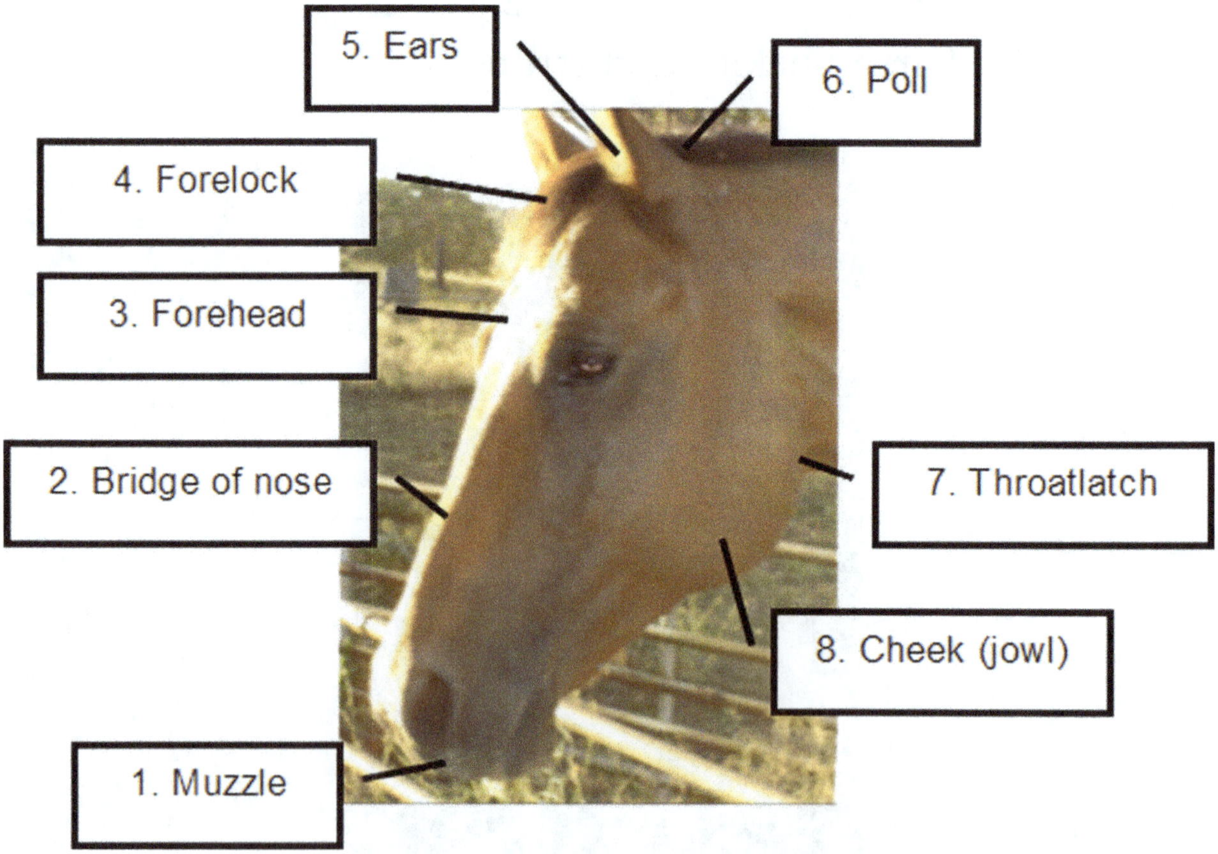

- 1. Muzzle
- 2. Bridge of nose
- 3. Forehead
- 4. Forelock
- 5. Ears
- 6. Poll
- 7. Throatlatch
- 8. Cheek (jowl)

Parts of the body – horse neck to rear

Say hello to Asha.

See what you can remember:

Parts of the body – Horse neck to rear. Point to the following parts of the horse:

1. Hoof
2. Knee
3. Shoulder
4. Neck
5. Mane / Crest
6. Withers
7. Back
8. Loin
9. Hip
10. Rump
11. Tail
12. Hock
13. Fetlock
14. Coronet
15. Flank

How to ride a horse

Point to the following parts of the horse head:

1. Muzzle
2. Bridge of nose
3. Forehead
4. Forelock
5. Ears
6. Poll
7. Throatlatch
8. Cheek

Notes

Lesson 12

Module – Horse Riding Skills Checklist

Things to remember:

1. Rise up and down at the trot at the correct speed with the beat of the hoof.

2. Good control of your horse once you are balanced and trotting freely on the correct diagonal.

3. Keeps hands low near the shoulders of the horse.

4. Elbows by your side.

5. Lifting chest up to sit straight, pushing shoulders down to keep arms and hands low.

6. Back straight and tucking tail bone under to sit deep into the saddle.

7. Knees bent is the secret. Heels down, toes up and in, pressure on the inside of your foot to push your thighs into the saddle.

8. Riding your horse with your bottom, thighs and top of calves is the SECRET to successful horse riding.

The more it feels natural and you don't have to think so much about every movement, the easier it will become.

PRACTICE = PERFECTION = EASY = FUN

Notes

Lesson 13

Module – Your Horse and You

Things to know

Name: _____

Father (Sire): _____

Mother (Dam): _____

Microchip: _____

Height: _____

Measured in hands (hh), each hand is 4 inches (10cm) and taken horizontal from the withers. E.g. 100cm(1m) = 10hh.

As a guide ponies are less than 14.2hh, a Galloway is a horse 14.2-15hh, a Hack is a Horse over 15hh.

Weight: _____

Can be measured with a special measure tape. Ponies 200-360kg, Horses 350-600kg, Heavy Horse 550-800kg

How to ride a horse

Age: _____

(A foal is under 1 and still getting milk from mum, a weanling is under 1 no longer getting milk from mum, a yearling is 1-2yrs, a filly and colt 2-3yrs, a mare and gelding or stallion from 4yrs+)

Gender: _____

(Filly and colt under 4yrs, mare, gelding, stallion 4+)

Breed: _____

Andalusian, Appaloosa, Australian Stock Horse (ASH), Australian Riding Pony, Arab, Brumby, Clydesdale or Draught, Friesian, Holsteiner, Lipizzaner, Miniature, Quarter Horse (QH), Paint or Pinto, Palomino, Piebald or Skewbald, Shetland, Standardbred, Thoroughbred, Waler, Warmblood, Welsh Pony.

Registration: _____

Brand: _____

*Usually two sets of numbers indicating the number of the foal and the birth year. Letters or symbols refer to the breeder or society. For instance: 14
  5

This means it is the fourteenth foal born in 2005 or 2015. Usually the horse will show its age sufficiently to tell us which decade it would be.

Markings: _____

You will generally see white points on a horse and they all have different terms such as:

LEGS: Coronet (small white line above hoof), Half Pastern (wide white marking above hoof), Sock (as it sounds), Stocking (like a long white sock from hoof to knee).

FACE: Star (between eyes), Blaze (between eyes to end of nose), Snip (white between nostrils), Bald (most front of face white), Stripe (thin white blaze like a line from eyes to nose).

Colour: _____

Good Reference – http://www.equusite.com/articles/basics/basicsColors.shtml

The basic colours you will see are Brown, Bay (brown with black mane and tail and usually a black strip on top of rump to tail), Black, Chestnut (red/orange with mane and tail same colour as coat), Flaxen is with a lighter mane and tail, Liver Chestnut is a very dark chestnut, White or Light grey are born white (variations from dapple grey to flea bitten with black sprinkled through the coat).

Other colours can be mixed with the name of a breed as well such as Cremellos (white mane and tail with pink skin), Roan (reddish and blue mix of colours with white), Palomino (golden with white mane and tail), Paint/Pinto (black and white is piebald and brown and white is skewbald), Appaloosa (looks like a leopard, white with dark spots).

Your Horse and You – Record List

Name: _____   Brand: _____

Father (Sire): _____   Markings: _____

Mother (Dam): _____   Colour: _____

Microchip: _____

Height: _____

Weight: _____

Age: _____

Gender: _____

Breed: _____

Registration: _____

Horse Healthcare Checklist

Name: _____

Last Drench: _____ (approx. every 8-12 weeks)

Last Shoeing: _____ (approx. every 5-7 weeks)

Last Tetanus/Strangles vaccination (equivac 2 in 1):

_____ (yearly)

Teeth: _____ (yearly)

Body work: _____

(chiropractor / acupuncture as needed)

Last Hendra vaccination

_____ (yearly)

Grooming Kit Essentials

Reasons for grooming a horse:
- To clean the horse, remove mud, sweat and old hair
- To notice any irregularities and injuries
- To stimulate blood flow to the skin for a healthier coat and muscle tone
- To improve overall appearance – healthy and shiny
- To bond with the horse

Basic necessities:
- Hoof pick
- Dandy brush – slightly harder for removing mud
- Curry comb – for removing mud and old hair and stimulates blood flow
- Body brush – slightly softer for all over to remove dust
- Sponges
- Mane comb
- Water brush
- Sweat scraper
- Small plastic bucket

Extras:

- Hoof oil and brush
- Bot knife
- Scissors
- Plait bands and tape
- Vaseline
- Hoof black-it for competitions

In review

You are going well with being able to understand basic control and rise trot with ease.

Your horse handling is excellent as is your ability to groom and saddle your own horse.

Your focus now is to get more assertiveness (firm but kind) making sure the horse knows what you want by your seat movements in the saddle and hand/leg controls. If leaning forward losing balance is a habit, you have to break it to improve.

To achieve a good canter you will need to practice a lot more sit trot, having strong leg muscles and good direction of the horse.

Giddy Up Beginner Books

Feeling confident in your mind is the most important thing. Strong instructions, predicting horse behaviour and feeling your horse is essential to move to the next level of your riding. The more it feels natural and you don't have to think so much about every movement, the easier it will become.

PRACTICE = PERFECTION = EASY = FUN

Notes

Lesson 14

Module – What next?

This is your time to work out with your instructor, your parents, your friend and yourself where you want to take your horse journey to provide a pathway that gives you enjoyment with horses. Decide whether to just to ride for fun, or keep developing your skills further to have more knowledge.

Intermediate Riding Skills

- The art of sit trot and cantering
- Bareback riding – balance and art
- Perfecting walk, trot and canter (techniques)
- Learn how to turn a horse on forehand/hindlegs

Advanced Riding Skills

- Perfecting walk, trot and canter (techniques)
- Learn how to turn/spin a horse on hindlegs
- How to get a horse to back up
- How to achieve head carriage for various riding disciplines
- Focus on discipline of interest

Advanced Horse Care

- Horse first aid basics
- Horse nutrition
- Horse care in the paddock
- Horse care in the stable
- Horse fitness
- Dentistry
- Acupuncture / Chiropractic
- Washing and clipping
- Pony Club and Show preparation
- Shoeing

Horsemanship and Training

- Catching and handling different horses
- Establishing confidence based on horse age, level of education, breed
- Floating
- Discipline vs kindness
- Training and education of horses in various riding disciplines

Giddy Up Beginner Books

Horse Pathway Development Guide

There is so much to know and learn, with an exciting journey through achievements. This guide is just a snapshot. The content and order in which you are taught can vary greatly when working with animals.

Experience the love, passion, energy and freedom of horses!

Foundation

Theory

Horse parts and saddlery
Safety tips

Horse Care and Handling

Horse sense
Confidence holding a horse
Leading

Riding Skills

Ground exercises
Mount and Dismount
Correct riding position – balance stand in stirrup
Emergency controls
Rein control at halt
Walk, stop, turn controls

Level 1 – Beginners

Theory

Horse parts and saddlery
Colours and breeds

Horse Care and Handling

Tie with Quick Release knot
Grooming basic

Riding Skills

Gear check
Mount and dismount drill
Mounted exercises
Rein control at walk
Transitions walk/halt/walk
Rider Aids
Arena circle patterns 10/20m/figure eight

Level 2 – Trotters

Theory

Horse parts and saddlery
Gender, colours and breeds

Horse Care and Handling

Put on a halter and 2 slip knots
Grooming kit usage and front feet pick up
Observation putting on saddle and bridle

Riding Skills

Mounted exercises at walk
Arena patterns serpentine and rein changes
Transitions walk/trot/walk
Rein control at trot
Sit trot and rise trot, correct diagonal
Hand technique and leg aids

Level 3 – Canters

Theory

Worming and shoeing frequency

Horse Care and Handling

Measure and weigh a horse
Catch horse in stable and rugging
Clean out hooves
Tack up saddle and bridle
Leading at trot, to side and back

Riding Skills

Correct trot diagonal, balanced horse and rider
Sit trot serpentines
Shorten and lengthen stride at trot
Canter basics
Intro to different disciplines jump poles, sporting, dressage
Inside and outside leg aid control

Level 4 – Advanced

Theory

Horse markings
Paddock management
Different types of bandages for jumping/first aid
Grooming care after riding

Horse Care and Handling

Catch horse in the paddock
Administer a wormer (calculated)
Bridle and saddle any type of horse
Put on bandages and leg boots

Riding Skills

Trail ride
Leg yield side pass, turns forehand and hind, backup
Flexing around circles
Transitions between walk to trot to canter to walk
Figure eight canter trot and walk changes / canter hand gallop
Bareback to trot
Dressage test
Jumping to 30cm

Level 5 – Advanced 2: Horsemanship

Theory

Hoof care, correct shoeing
Different bits and saddles
First aid treatments (colic, rainscald, wounds, antibiotics)
Feed and Nutrition, body weight score, read a brand
Use of lunging gear (roller, side reins)

Horse Care and Handling

Pull off a shoe
Pull apart saddle
Making up feeds
Floating and towing
Lunging walk/trot/canter, square stand

Riding Skills

Canter on request from any gait, complex changes
Leg yield spins, side pass, back up and adapt to discipline
One handed riding walk/trot/canter and open gate
Horse training and head carriage (running rein, double rein)
Riding with speed control collected and extended
Bareback to canter
Jump to 60cm (cross, double, course)
Natural horsemanship, connection/energy work

How to ride a horse

It is highly recommended to take the time to learn the basics of horse care, handling and riding preparation before stepping into the world of riding, but sometimes, due to cost and time constraint, this is not achievable for most without their own horse.

Please take care in your journey to learn safely with an experienced coach and well-trained horse to ensure positive outcomes.

Giddy Up Beginner Books

UNTIL NEXT TIME... RIDE, RELAX, ENJOY

I wish you happiness and health always!

Learn more and feel better with equine energy!

LOVE, LAUGH, LIVE

DANCE AND SING

SHARE YOUR LIGHT

RUN FREE WITH HORSES

Debbie Burgermeister

About the Author

Debbie has been blessed with a loving family, an upbringing on a farm, learning practical life skills, and many great horsemanship skills from a very talented horseman. Her father, who taught her to break-in horses thirty years ago in the natural way, and to be able to ride horses to compete up to state level championships. Starting with pony club and moving into the show ring, dressage, jumping, campdrafting, barrel racing and polocrosse, she was a member of the breathtaking 2000 Olympics opening ceremony team of one hundred and twenty musical ride performers.

Debbie is your coach with a difference, through her ability to achieve a high focus on development with strong attention to technique from exposure to both Western and English riding. She has run an established riding school since 2006, and has many coaching qualifications, but her unique qualities come from her down-to-earth, friendly, positive attitude and ability to relate to all ages. She is a parent of twins and understands the high expectations of child development in recreational activities. Debbie's life is now completely dedicated to her family, her horses, and the charity that she and her husband, Mark, founded, called Giddy Up Gold Coast. Providing horse experiences through her horse riding school Bonogin Valley Horse Retreat, aimed at the grassroots of the sport, which is passionate about the healing aspects of horses for the community.

Deb's vision is to provide beginner horse enthusiasts across the world with a guided education pathway. Providing the best start to horse riding through her resources.

A mission for beginner horse lovers to have an easier and safer start to their horse riding journey and reduce the risks of getting hurt. To enjoy learning, grow in confidence and have foundation knowledge for horse ownership.

The amazing world of horses provides development in confidence, nonverbal communication techniques, and emotional control, along with an escape from technology and getting back to nature to unplug and unwind. Together with the mental and physical strength to handle life's challenges and to experience the energy, love, and freedom that horses can provide.

Be a part of a Horse Lovers Community and guided with your journey at www.horseridinghub.com.au. Development of confidence, care and communication is the blessing we wish you for a happy and healthy life.

Author Certifications

Equestrian Australia coach
CertIII Sports Coaching Equestrian
CertIV Trainer and Assessor
Senior First Aid, Mental Health First Aid and Blue Card
CertIV in Small Business Management
Advanced Diploma of Customer Contact Management

Further Information and Contact Details

Horse Riding Hub
info@horseridinghub.com.au
www.horseridinghub.com.au

Giddy Up Beginner Books

GIDDY UP BEGINNER BOOKS

Collect The Series

Easy to read for kids and adults

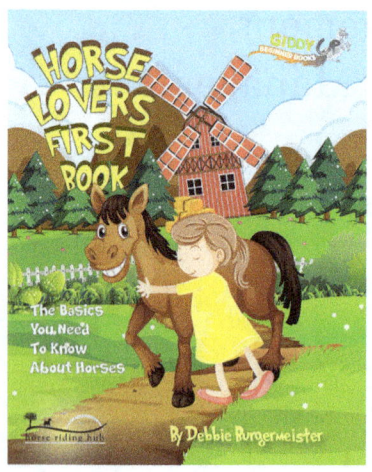  

HORSE LOVERS FIRST BOOK: A first horse book filled with colour, horse cartoons, photos and answers to the very basics you need to know about horses.

HOW TO RIDE A HORSE: Riding Lessons for Beginners Workbook as a step-by-step education resource. With a bonus development guide for parents.

READY FOR YOUR FIRST HORSE?: Read this first! An expert's guide when looking for a beginners horse for sale. Essential checklists for everything you need to find out before owning a horse.

Become a Horse Lover Member!

Find out how at
www.horseridinghub.com/membershub

AN EDUCATION PATHWAY

Horse Lovers Worldwide

Horses are our heritage! Help keep horses a part of our community, to run free with these amazing animals. Experience the joy and freedom they bring into your life and the lives of those around you.

A resource for beginner horse lovers, to obtain quality information and education for a safer horse journey.

www.ingramcontent.com/pod-product-compliance
Lightning Source LLC
Chambersburg PA
CBHW060534010526
44107CB00059B/2636